GREAT RIVERS

The
YANGTZE

Michael Pollard

BENCHMARK BOOKS

MARSHALL CAVENDISH
NEW YORK

Benchmark Books
Marshall Cavendish Corporation
99 White Plains Road
Tarrytown, New York 10591

American edition © Marshall Cavendish Corporation 1998

First published in 1997 by Evans Brothers Limited
© Evans Brothers Limited 1997

Library of Congress Cataloging-in-Publication Data
Pollard, Michael, date.
    The Yangtze / Michael Pollard.
        p. cm. — (Great rivers)
    Includes bibliographical references and index.
    Summary: Traces the course of the third longest river
in the world, the Yangtze in China, and describes its
physical features, history, importance as a source of food
and for transportation, and more.
    ISBN 0-7614-0505-4 (lib. bdg.)
    1. Yangtze River (China)—Description and travel—
Juvenile literature. 2. Yangtze River Valley (China)—
Description and travel—Juvenile literature. [1. Yangtze
River] I. Title. II. Series: Pollard, Michael, date.
Great rivers.
DS793.Y3P64 1998
951'.2—DC21   97-3539
                                                    CIP
                                                    AC

Printed in Hong Kong

ACKNOWLEDGEMENTS

For permission to reproduce copyright material, the author
and publishers gratefully acknowledge the following:

Cover (main image) Image Bank (bottom left) Hans
Reinhard/Bruce Coleman Ltd (bottom right) Hutchison
Library
Title page Gilidicelli/Hutchison Library
page 8 Image Bank **page 9** DRA/Still Pictures **page 10**
James Davis Travel Photography **page 11** Image Bank **page
12** Victoria and Albert Museum/Bridgeman Art Library
page 13 Hutchison Library **page 14** China National
Tourist Board **page 15** Image Bank/China Tourism Photo
page 16 Robert Harding Picture Library **page 17** (top)
Panos Pictures/Alain Le Garsmeur (bottom) Eye Ubiquitous/
Julia Waterlow **page 18** James Davis Travel Photography
page 19 Wang Gang Feng/Panos Pictures **page 20** Robert
Harding Picture Library **page 21** (top left) Trip/M Watson
(top right) Robert Harding Picture Library **page 22** Mary
Evans Picture Library **page 23** Robert Harding Picture
Library **page 24** Trip/M Watson **page 25** (left) Jeffrey
Aaronson/Network Aspen/Colorific (right) Panos Pictures
page 26 Jeffrey Aaronson/Network Aspen/Colorific

page 27 (top) Jardine Matheson and Company Ltd (bottom)
Image Bank **page 28** Panos Pictures/Alain Le Garsmeur
page 29 (top left) Robert Harding Picture Library (bottom)
Alain Le Garsmeur/Panos Pictures **page 30** Earth Satellite
Corporation/Science Photo Library **page 31** Chine
Nouvelle-Sipa Press/Rex Features **page 32** Atlantide/Bruce
Coleman Ltd **page 33** (top left) Gordon D. R. Clements/
Axiom (top right) Atlantide/Bruce Coleman Ltd **page 34**
Chine Nouvelle-Sipa Press/Rex Features **page 35** Jim
Holmes/Axiom **page 36** Trip/F Good **page 37** (top) Image
Bank (bottom) James Davis Travel Photography **page 38**
Catherine Platt/Panos Pictures **page 39** (top) Image Bank
(middle) Ecoscene/Alan Towse (bottom) Gordon D. R.
Clements/Axiom **page 40** Hans Reinhard/Bruce Coleman
Ltd **page 41** (top) Hans Reinhard/Bruce Coleman Ltd
(bottom) Nigel Sitwell/ Hutchison Library **page 42**
Kvaerner Cleveland Bridge **page 43** (top) Chris
Stowers/Panos Pictures (bottom) Andree Kaiser/Rex
Features

CONTENTS

THE GREAT RIVER

THE YANGTZE IS THE THIRD LONGEST RIVER IN THE WORLD. ONLY THE NILE IN AFRICA AND THE AMAZON IN SOUTH AMERICA ARE LONGER.

THE CHINESE HAVE THEIR OWN NAMES for different sections of the Yangtze's course. They call the whole river Chang Jiang, which means simply "Great River." They use the name "Yangtze" only for the lower part, where the river flows towards the East China Sea. This was the first section that became known to Europeans, and so, outside China, the whole river was called the Yangtze. The name "Yangtze" is used in this book, but in atlases and other books you may find the river called the Yangzi, the Chang Jiang or the Yangtse Kiang.

FERTILE PLAIN

The Yangtze flows for 3988 miles (6418 kilometers) from its source on the borders of China and Tibet to the China Sea. On the way it is joined by 700 tributaries, some of which are themselves major rivers. It collects water from an area of 755,984 square miles (1,958,000 square kilometers), which is about the same as the area of Germany, France, Italy and Spain combined. The wide, fertile plain of the lower Yangtze and the hot, wet summers make it good farming land. About 7000 years ago, travelers from the valley of the Huang Ho, or Yellow River, in northern China were driven south by hostile tribes from the mountains of Mongolia. They settled on the plain and learned how to irrigate the

QINGHAI

▲ Mt. Gelandandong

TIBET

Yangtze

◀ Looking down on the Yangtze at Chongqing, China's largest city. The Yangtze is joined from the right by the Jialing, one of its longest tributaries. The tall building on the left is a pagoda, a Buddhist temple.

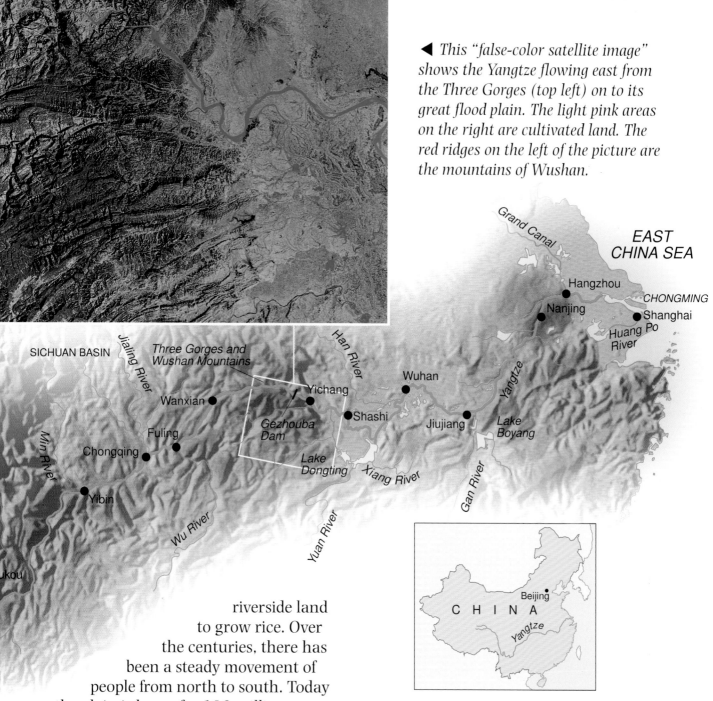

◀ *This "false-color satellite image" shows the Yangtze flowing east from the Three Gorges (top left) on to its great flood plain. The light pink areas on the right are cultivated land. The red ridges on the left of the picture are the mountains of Wushan.*

EAST CHINA SEA

Grand Canal

Hangzhou

Nanjing

CHONGMING

Shanghai

Huang Po River

SICHUAN BASIN

Jialing River

Three Gorges and Wushan Mountains

Han River

Wuhan

Yangtze

Min River

Wanxian

Yichang

Gezhouba Dam

Shashi

Jiujiang

Lake Boyang

Fuling

Chongqing

Lake Dongting

Xiang River

Gan River

Yibin

Wu River

Yuan River

Dukou

Beijing

C H I N A

Yangtze

riverside land to grow rice. Over the centuries, there has been a steady movement of people from north to south. Today the plain is home for 193 million people, about twenty per cent of China's total population.

NORTH AND SOUTH

The Yangtze marks the boundary between two different ways of life. In northern China, where the climate is temperate and it can be very cold in winter, the main food is wheat, maize or millet. Along the Yangtze and to the south, where the summers are hot and wet and the winters are short, rice is grown for food.

THE YANGTZE

Length: 3988 mi (6418 km)
Source: Mount Gelandandong, Qinghai Province
Mouth: Shanghai
Main tributaries:
 Yalong 737 mi (1187 km); joins at Dukou, Sichuan
 Min 493 mi (793 km); joins at Yibin, Sichuan
 Jialing 695 mi (1119 km); joins at Chongqing, Sichuan
 Wu 633 mi (1018 km); joins at Fuling, Sichuan
 Yuan 617 mi (993 km); joins at Lake Dongting, Hunan
 Xiang 504 mi (811 km); joins at Lake Dongting, Hunan
 Han 952 mi (1532 km); joins at Wuhan, Hubei
 Gan 471 mi (758 km); joins at Jiujiang, Jianxi
 Huang Po 71 mi (114 km); joins near Shanghai

THE MAKING OF A RIVER

OVER 100 MILLION YEARS AGO
MOVEMENTS IN THE EARTH'S CRUST
STARTED TO FORM THE YANGTZE.

TODAY'S CONTINENTS AND OCEANS were being formed as sections of the crust, or outer layer, of the Earth moved together or apart. One section, or crustal plate, covered most of present-day Europe and Asia. Another stretched southeastwards from India as far as Australia and New Zealand.

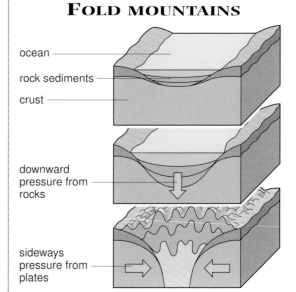

FOLD MOUNTAINS

ocean

rock sediments

crust

downward pressure from rocks

sideways pressure from plates

1 Rock sediments collect on the ocean floor and are compressed into a solid mass.

2 The Earth's crust sinks under the weight of the rock.

3 The crustal plates are pushed together and the rock layers are pushed upwards to form fold mountains.

◀ *Intensive cultivation on the banks of the Yangtze in Sichuan Province. The hillside has been terraced to improve drainage and make more land available for growing fruit and vegetables.*

These two plates moved towards each other. When they collided, they pushed up ranges of fold mountains across northern India, Nepal, Bhutan, Tibet and northwestern China. The process of change and movement in the Earth's crust is still happening today.

In winter, icy winds, often below -20°F (-30°C), sweep over the mountains from northern Asia. Just below its surface the land is frozen all year round. In China's Qinghai province, north of Tibet, streams flow from the glaciers and melting snow and come together to form the Yangtze. The river finds its way out of the mountains down deep gorges and along steep-sided valleys.

EROSION

As the water rushes down from the mountains, it brings with it pieces of the softer rocks that have been worn away. This process is called erosion. When the river slows down, the pieces of rock fall to the river bed. There the action of the water grinds the rock into smaller pieces and eventually into sand and mud. Some of this is light enough to be picked up again by the water and carried downstream. When the water slows down again, the material is deposited once more. Tributaries of the Yangtze carry more deposits to add to the ones already on the river bed.

This happens in two stages. First, material from the mountains of western China is carried down to the Sichuan Basin. It is deposited there as the river slows down. Then, in eastern Sichuan, the river cuts its way through a series of ravines and gorges. As it picks up speed, it gathers more material from its banks. This is deposited downstream where the land is flatter and the river slows again. The action of the water on the particles of sand on the river bed grinds them down even smaller. By the time it reaches the delta, near the mouth of the river, the deposit is more like mud. Every year, 1.6 billion tons of deposits are carried down the Yangtze.

FLOOD DANGER

The two areas of deposits, in the Sichuan Basin and in the lower Yangtze valley down to the East China Sea, are rich, fertile farming land. However, the Yangtze can burst its banks and flood the surrounding land, ruining crops and sometimes bringing death and disaster to riverside towns and villages. For well over 2000 years, the people of the Yangtze valley have been striving to control flooding, and the struggle continues today.

▲ *As the Yangtze leaves the mountains of western China, it is joined by mountain streams like this one, which pours spectacularly over the Luorelong Falls in western Sichuan.*

THE YANGTZE IN HISTORY

PEOPLE FIRST BEGAN TO SETTLE AND FARM
IN THE YANGTZE VALLEY ABOUT
9000 YEARS AGO.

BY ABOUT 3000 BC people were living in large villages, often protected from attackers and flood water by banks of earth. The main crop was rice, grown in paddy fields – fields that had been flooded with water channeled from the river. When the rice grain was harvested, the plants were used to feed pigs and chickens.

The early settlers along the Yangtze were the target of constant attacks from the north. The invaders looked with envy on the rich farming land of the river valley. They were skilled horsemen and fierce warriors. The more peaceable southern Chinese were no match for them.

▲ *The Grand Canal 200 years ago. Besides being an important trading route between the Yangtze and northern China, it was also used by the pleasure boats of the Imperial family.*

INVASION AND CIVIL WAR

The invaders set up their own states and then began to fight among themselves. This pattern was repeated over and over again through many centuries until, in 221 BC, China became one country for the first time. Its rulers became rich and powerful, living in splendid palaces, but they also spent vast sums of money on big construction projects. It was during this time that China's famous Great Wall, close to its northern border, was built.

The Yangtze valley was a vital source of

12

◀ *After years of neglect, the Grand Canal is once again in use as a commercial waterway. These barges are moored at Hangzhou at the Canal's southern end, close to its meeting with the Yangtze.*

THE GRAND CANAL

In AD 578, Emperor Yang Ti ordered work to start on a canal linking the trading city of Hangzhou, 186 miles (300 kilometers) from the mouth of the Yangtze, with Beijing 1554 miles (2500 kilometers) away to the north. Five million men were employed on the project. Almost half of them died from overwork or starvation. When it was finished, it was called the Grand Canal, or sometimes the Great, or Imperial, Canal. It was neglected and became blocked by silt in the nineteenth century, but it was cleared and repaired in the 1980s and there are plans to extend it further northwards.

RICH AND POOR

To China's peasant population, working on the land along the Yangtze and the Huang Ho, it made little difference who was in power. Their lives were made up of hard work and terrible poverty. If there were floods or a drought, they starved. If there were good harvests, their crops were taken and sold by the landowners. There was nothing they could do to improve their lives. There were two Chinese nations. One was the nation of rulers in their palaces, surrounded by riches. The other was the nation of peasants, spending their lives in back-breaking toil and earning little for it. Peasants either worked for a farmer for very low pay or had to pay high rents for land that they worked themselves. Rulers came and went, but little changed for most ordinary Chinese people until the middle of the twentieth century.

food for the heavily populated cities of north-eastern China. The first emperors of China were keen to increase the Yangtze's food crops and they ordered more land to be watered from the river. They also built canals to provide a route for supply ships from the Yangtze to the Huang Ho, China's other great river to the north. The longest canal, which is still the longest in the world, was the Grand Canal. It took twenty years to build.

TALES OF THE YANGTZE

FOR THOUSANDS OF YEARS, THE LIVES OF PEOPLE ALONG THE YANGTZE VALLEY HAVE CENTERED ON THE RIVER. IT CAN BRING THEM GOOD HARVESTS OR STARVATION, FLOODING AND DEATH. SO IT IS NOT SURPRISING THAT MANY STORIES ARE TOLD ABOUT THE RIVER.

PRINCESS YAO JI

AT THE WITCHES' GORGE near Wushan the Yangtze flows for 25 miles (40 kilometers) between steep cliffs. Above the cliffs are six mountains on each side. One of these is the Goddess Peak, whose shape resembles a kneeling figure. The kneeling figure is said to be the Princess Yao Ji. The story goes that she loved the river and the mountains so much that she decided to live there forever with eleven maidens – the other eleven mountains – to look after her. They kept watch to protect sailors from the dangerous waters of the Gorge and to prevent floods from damaging the Yangtze peasants' crops.

▲ *The Goddess Peak, on the right, towers over the Yangtze at the Witches' Gorge.*

THE TIGER GENERAL

Zhang Fei was a soldier in Sichuan in the second century AD. He was famous for his cruelty and was known as the "Tiger General." His cruelty won him enemies, two of whom attacked him, cut off his head and threw it in the Yangtze near the city of Yunyang. A fisherman was sailing nearby. He saw Zhang Fei's head floating in the water and dreamed that the Tiger General asked him to rescue his head and give it a proper burial. The fisherman obeyed, and a temple now stands where the head was buried. Yangtze sailors used to believe that in return for the fisherman's kindness, Zhang Fei's spirit changed into a helpful wind to get ships out of trouble in stormy weather.

THE BATTLE OF THE RED CLIFF

The Battle of the Red Cliff was a real battle that took place in AD 208 on Lake Dongting in Hunan. It was between the kingdoms of Wei and Shu, two of the three kingdoms of China at that time. The Wei general, Cao Cao, assembled a huge army of 200,000 men and planned to attack the Shu forces across the lake. But his men were not used to naval warfare and were nervous. A Shu spy persuaded Cao Cao to tie his warships together so that the soldiers would feel safer. When morning came, the Shu forces set fire to the Wei ships with burning arrows, and Cao Cao had to retreat.

The Red Cliffs are said to have been scorched red by the burning ships, and the victorious Shu general celebrated by writing *Chi Bi* (Red Cliff) on the cliff face. The writing can still be seen today.

THE GREEDY MONK

Shibaozhai is a twelve-story pavilion that stands beside a sheer 722-foot (220-meter) cliff above the Yangtze in Sichuan. Inside, a spiral staircase leads to a monastery at the top of the cliff, which has a strange legend attached to it.

One of the duties of the monks was to pray for the safety of boats sailing along the Yangtze. In return for this their gods supplied them with free rice which poured out of a hole in the rocks nearby.

There was always just enough rice each day for the monks and their visitors, but this was not enough for one greedy monk. He decided to make the hole bigger and sell the surplus rice that flowed out. This so angered the gods that they immediately stopped the supply of rice. What was worse, they refused to listen to the monks' prayers for the Yangtze sailors and they gave them no more protection from rocks and storms. And from that moment on, this section of the river became notorious for shipwrecks.

◄ *The monastery at Shibaozhai is over 250 years old, but the pavilion was added in 1819, giving the monks easier access from the river. Before that, they had to haul themselves up the sheer cliff-face with the help of an iron chain.*

THE SOURCE OF THE YANGTZE

THE YANGTZE STARTS ITS JOURNEY ON THE QINGHAI PLATEAU OF NORTHWESTERN CHINA, ON THE BORDER WITH TIBET. THIS IS ONE OF THE MOST REMOTE PLACES ON EARTH.

THE MOUNTAINS OF THE QINGHAI PLATEAU are capped with snow and ice for most of the year. The meltwaters of the Plateau flow south and east. The exact source of the Yangtze was a mystery until, in 1976, a scientific expedition traced it to the slopes of Mount Gelandandong, 21,722 feet (6621 meters) high. There, melting glaciers and snow form the streams that are the true beginnings of the Yangtze.

YAKS AND YURTS

In the short summer months from late May to August, water trickles from the melting snowcaps and glaciers. It crosses landscapes covered with rock debris brought down by the water or by frost action. The trickles form small streams, combine with others and slowly increase in size. This is very remote country where few outsiders are ever seen. On the lower slopes of the plateau, sheltered from the bitterest weather, live nomadic herdsmen and their families. They move from place to place in search of grazing for their animals. Their homes are yurts – tents made of yak-hides or felt. They keep yaks for milk as well as for transport, together with sheep and sometimes goats. When winter approaches they bring their animals down to lower streams because the water freezes on higher slopes. In the most sheltered spots they grow a hardy kind of barley, which they grind into flour as their basic food.

▲ *The mountains of Tibet. In spring, their melting snows and glaciers feed streams that combine to form the Yangtze. The well-trodden right bank of this stream shows that a herd of animals has recently watered here.*

FLOWING SOUTH

Below about 9842 feet (3000 meters), the rivers flow through broader valleys and in and out of lakes. They leave behind on their banks deposits of fine sand brought down from the mountains. Life is a little easier here. There are villages of timber huts, with fields of barley beside the water.

For about 497 miles (800 kilometers), the Yangtze heads southwards on a winding course through narrow valleys. At one point, it looks as if it is going to force its way through the mountains to join up with the Mekong river and continue southwards through Vietnam to the sea. Millions of years ago it did take this route. But now it loops back on itself, then back again, and ends up flowing northeast. This part of the river is in a region that until about 50 years ago was almost completely cut off from the rest of China. Its people lived a tribal life under their own local rulers, who were often Buddhist priests. But gradually, with the building of railways and roads through this difficult country, the old way of life changed and is still changing today. However, some settlements can still be reached only along mountain pathways and across rope bridges.

BUILDING A YURT

Yurts are ideal homes for nomadic people who are often on the move. They can be quickly assembled or easily dismantled and turned into a neat bundle for a pack animal to carry. Yurts are round and measure about 16 feet (five meters) across. The inner wall is a latticework of thin willow boughs bound together so that it can be rolled and unrolled. Screens made of woven reeds are tied to this frame. Thicker boughs form the roof supports, which are then covered with several layers of felt or yak-hides. An iron stove with a central chimney keeps the yurt warm at night.

▲ *The mountains of north-western China are home to about 800,000 nomadic Kazak people. This family has set up its yurt for the summer high in the mountains.*

◀ *When autumn comes, they will move lower down, loading their belongings on their yaks.*

THE SICHUAN BASIN

As the Yangtze runs northeast it flows around a great plain, the Sichuan Basin, sometimes called the "Red Basin" because of the red sandstone hills surrounding it. The Sichuan Basin is home to about 100 million people, or ten per cent of China's total population.

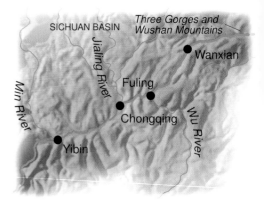

The Sichuan Basin is where four rivers meet. They are the Yangtze itself, which flows along the southern edge of the Basin, the Min and Jialing tributaries, which flow in from the north, and the Wu from the south. Millions of years ago, the Basin was a gulf, or inlet, of the present Pacific Ocean and then, after upheavals of the Earth's crust, it became a freshwater lake. Later movements of the crust formed the mountains to the north, south and west, and drained the lake. This explains the richness of the soil. As the lake flowed away, it left behind muddy deposits and mineral salts.

◀ A traditional ferry makes its way across the Yangtze in Sichuan. Away from major cities, there are few bridges across the Yangtze and ferries play an important part in the local communications network.

Although it is, on average, 1640 feet (500 meters) above sea-level, the Sichuan Basin is sheltered by mountains. Its winters are mild, and it has a long, warm rainy season in summer. Taking advantage of this climate, settlers began to control its rivers with dams and irrigation channels over 2500 years ago. Crops are grown for about eleven months of the year, with new plantings following closely after each harvest. The main crop is rice, and the flooded paddy fields produce two harvests every year. Other crops include rape-seed for edible oil, mulberry trees as food for silkworms, sugar cane, cotton, jute, fruit and vegetables.

The hillsides surrounding the Basin are an important source of timber, and the lower slopes are used as pasture for herd animals.

ENERGY RESOURCES

Until the twentieth century, the Sichuan Basin was almost cut off from the rest of China behind the barriers of the mountains. The Yangtze was the main link with the rest of

MINERALS ON THE YANGTZE

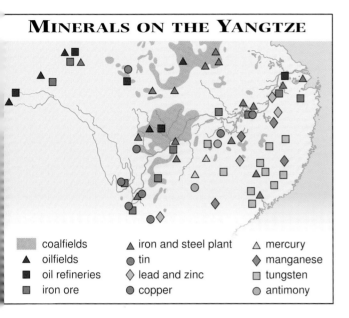

▨ coalfields	▲ iron and steel plant	△ mercury
▲ oilfields	● tin	◆ manganese
■ oil refineries	◇ lead and zinc	▢ tungsten
▢ iron ore	● copper	◐ antimony

▼ *Although religion is discouraged by the Chinese government, the Buddhist faith still survives in remote areas of China such as western Sichuan. These Buddhist priests, or lamas, are on their way to worship.*

China, but rocks, reefs and narrow gorges made the journey by river slow and dangerous. Yet the rest of China needed food from Sichuan's rich soil and the coal, iron ore, oil and natural gas buried underground.

Development of Sichuan began in the 1950s with the building of major new roads and railways. In 1970, work began on the Gezhouba Dam, on the Yangtze just east of the Sichuan border. The dam, then the largest in China, is 230 feet (70 meters) high and 1.6 miles (2.6 kilometers) wide, and took eighteen years to complete. It supplies water to 21 hydro-electric generators, which produce electricity for eastern Sichuan and as far away as Shanghai. But, large though it is, the Gezhouba Dam cannot compare with the huge Three Gorges Project (see pages 24–25), which will bring massive changes to life in the Sichuan Basin.

CITY OF CHANGE

HIGH ABOVE THE YANGTZE, OVERLOOKING THE RIVER
AND THE SICHUAN BASIN, IS
CHINA'S LARGEST CITY, CHONGQING.

THE YANGTZE IS JOINED AT CHONGQING by one of its major tributaries, the Jialing, which has its source 695 miles (1119 kilometers) away in the mountains to the northwest. The old city of Chongqing, surrounded by a 108-foot (33-meter) high wall, dates back to the fourth century BC. Built on the clifftops and with water around three sides, it is a natural fortress.

CONTRASTS

For 2500 years Chongqing has been a collection point for cargoes brought down the Yangtze and the Jialing. Besides the farming produce of Sichuan, Chongqing also traded in hides, wool, iron, copper, salt and

▲ *The Jialing river, in the foreground, flows from the north to meet the Yangtze at Chongqing. The Chinese government has chosen Chongqing as a center of industry and trade for southwestern China.*

even rhubarb. After the first steamship reached the port in 1898 it became even more important.

But there were still few modern facilities in the city. As late as the 1930s, Chongqing had no piped water supply, despite having grown to a population of 600,000 people. Thousands of water-carriers brought water up from the river in buckets. The water was often polluted, and outbreaks of water-borne diseases such as typhoid were common. There was no wheeled

THE GROWTH OF CHONGQING

The chance of work and housing are the two magnets that pull families towards large cities all over the world. Unlike many growing cities in Africa and South America, Chongqing has no run-down shanty towns of temporary homes on its outskirts. People who move there are properly housed and can find work in the newly developed industries.

▲ Rubbish piles up outside buildings in Chongqing. Waste disposal in a crowded city is always a problem. In the cities along the Yangtze, it is often taken away by barge to be dumped.

▶ These high-rise apartments represent the new face of Chongqing, set to expand even more over the next twenty years. Unlike most Chinese cities, Chongqing has few bicycles. The streets are too steep.

transport because the streets were so steep. People were carried about in sedan chairs and goods were carried on porters' backs. There were no bridges across the Yangtze or Jialing rivers. The only crossings were by ferry.

MODERN CHONGQING

Today, the Chongqing of the 1930s is part of history. Things began to change in 1938 during the war between China and Japan. Invading Japanese troops, advancing up the Yangtze, forced the Chinese government to set up its capital in Chongqing. Industries and universities too retreated there. Soon, the city had outgrown its old boundaries and spread to the hills on each side. It continued to grow after the government moved to Beijing in 1949. Chongqing's population is now fifteen million. Modern bridges cross both rivers, and

there are also two cablecars across the Jialing. Broad avenues link the districts of the enlarged city and the airport 15 miles (25 kilometers) to the west.

In the 1970s the government named Chongqing as one of the seven areas in China where industrial growth was to be concentrated. Machine tool works, silk and cotton mills and chemical factories were built, and in the last fifteen years they have been followed by newer industries, such as electronics and the manufacture of household electrical goods.

But Chongqing's prosperity has always been held back by its isolation. The Three Gorges downstream limit the size of ships that can come upriver, and mountains to the east make a direct east-west road or rail link difficult. This is the background to the Three Gorges Project (see pages 24–25), which will open up Chongqing to larger ships.

THE THREE GORGES

As the Yangtze leaves Sichuan, it forces its way eastwards through a range of mountains that the Chinese call Wushan.

In the mountains, the Three Gorges – Qutang, Wu and Xiling – extend along 118 miles (190 kilometers) of the river. In some places the river plunges through gaps in the limestone rocks that are only 328 feet (100 meters) wide. The water storms and swirls, stirring up sediment from the river bed and turning a muddy brown.

The Qutang Gorge, which is about 6 miles (ten kilometers) long, is the first and the shortest gorge. Then there is a stretch of quieter water before the river enters Wu Gorge, which is 25 miles (40 kilometers) long with vertical cliff sides. Finally, the Yangtze zig-zags down

▲ *A nineteenth-century European visitor's view of the Yangtze gorges. The Wushan mountains are in the background. On the far bank, a procession leads an important visitor to the palace on the hilltop.*

the rapids of Xiling Gorge for 47 miles (76 kilometers). The rapids are the result of rock falls caused over thousands of years by the action of rain and frost on the limestone of the Three Gorges. When rain is driven into cracks in the rock and then freezes, pieces of rock split off and crash to the river.

DANGEROUS WATERS

For centuries the Three Gorges, with their dangerous currents and whirlpools, rocks and rapids, were a serious block on trade from Sichuan. The gorges were hazardous for shipping at any time of the year. When the water level was low, rocks and reefs were exposed, which was dangerous for the ships. In the rainy season, the pressure and volume of water had to be overcome. Junks had to be dragged upstream by teams of "trackers." Usually about 100 men, but sometimes as many as 300, hauled boats up the river against the current with ropes of twisted bamboo that were 1312 feet (400 meters) long. Narrow paths for the trackers, linked by steep flights of steps, were cut into the cliff faces high above the water level. A huge

▼ *Coal barges face a choppy journey as they pass upstream through Xiling Gorge. Ahead of them are 93 miles (150 kilometers) of difficult water.*

amount of effort was needed by the trackers. Sometimes the ropes would break, the junk would slide back, and many hours of hard work would be wasted. Every year one junk in ten failed to complete the journey. Even when the first steamship sailed up the Yangtze in 1898, it had to be hauled through the Three Gorges by trackers. It could take more than a month to cover 249 miles (400 kilometers) of the Yangtze through the Gorges.

CLEARING THE WAY

As steamships grew in size, they became too big for even the largest and most skilled teams of trackers to handle. In 1898, explosives were used to clear the more dangerous rocks and rapids from the river bed. This reduced the hazards and the sailing time, but the voyage was never easy. When the Three Gorges Project is complete, Yangtze shipping will bypass the Gorges.

THE THREE GORGES PROJECT

THE THREE GORGES DAM IS THE LARGEST ENGINEERING PROJECT EVER PLANNED IN CHINA. WHEN THE PROJECT IS COMPLETED IN 2013, IT WILL HAVE CHANGED THE LIVES OF MILLIONS OF PEOPLE ALONG THE YANGTZE.

WORK BEGAN ON THE THREE GORGES DAM IN 1993. It is being built about 27 miles (43 kilometers) upstream from Yichang, near the border between the provinces of Sichuan and Hubei. It will be 574 feet (175 meters) high and 1.5 miles (2.4 kilometers) wide. Behind it, the dammed waters of the Yangtze will form a reservoir that will stretch 394 miles (634 kilometers) upstream to Chongqing.

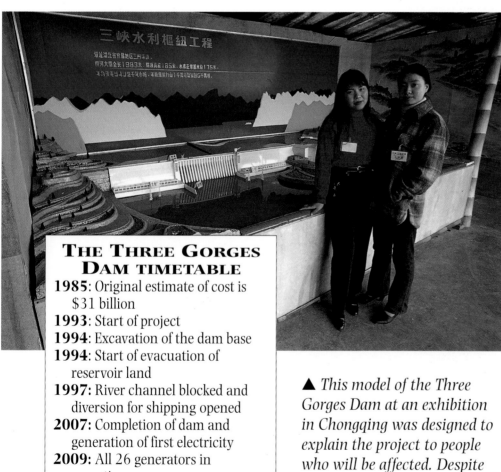

THE THREE GORGES DAM TIMETABLE

1985: Original estimate of cost is $31 billion

1993: Start of project

1994: Excavation of the dam base

1994: Start of evacuation of reservoir land

1997: River channel blocked and diversion for shipping opened

2007: Completion of dam and generation of first electricity

2009: All 26 generators in operation

2013: All work finally completed on project

▲ *This model of the Three Gorges Dam at an exhibition in Chongqing was designed to explain the project to people who will be affected. Despite all the publicity, however, many Chinese are not convinced of the advantages.*

DROWNED CITIES

The waters of the reservoir will cover thirteen existing towns and cities. Their inhabitants will have to move to new homes already being built on the hillsides. Two-thirds of the important silk-weaving city of Wanxian will be flooded, and 800,000 people will have to be moved. The lower parts of Chongqing will also disappear under water. People moved from the other cities and from farming villages will bring the total who have to move to 1.3 million. Farmers will have to leave their fertile, irrigated land by the river and start farming again on less rich, less well-drained land.

THREE AIMS

The Three Gorges Project has three aims. First, it is a hydroelectric plant, by far the largest in the world. When its 26 generators are in full operation, producing electricity as water flows through their turbines, they will provide about ten per cent of eastern and central China's energy needs well into the next century.

Second, the dam will control the waters of the Yangtze, releasing them slowly and preventing floods along the lower river. Third, ships will bypass the dam in a series of fourteen locks or be carried over it in "ship elevators." Ocean-going ships up to 10,000 tons will be able to dock at Chongqing.

FOR AND AGAINST

There are fierce arguments inside and outside China about the Three Gorges Project. Some scientists fear that it will end in disaster. The dam might break, sending a torrent of water downstream and drowning thousands of people. It might be a target in any future war. The weight of the dam and its reservoir might trigger disturbances underground and cause earthquakes. There are worries, too, about the loss of endangered species of plants and animals living in the area to be flooded, and about the escalating cost of the project. The cost is already four times the 1985 estimate – enough to build six Channel Tunnels.

Other experts say that these fears are groundless and that the benefits of the project will be huge. China needs the electricity that will be generated, Sichuan needs the jobs and prosperity that better access up the Yangtze will bring, and millions of people living downstream will be spared the fear of floods.

▲ A Wanxian family, whose old home will disappear under the waters of the Three Gorges reservoir, prepares to move. A new city is being built higher in the mountains for 800,000 Wanxian people.

◄ This channel is being cut to divert ships around the site of the Three Gorges Dam while it is under construction. When the project is completed, the channel will be replaced by a series of locks.

THE FLOOD PLAIN

THE MIDDLE COURSE OF THE YANGTZE COVERS THE 621 MILES (1000 KILOMETERS) DOWNSTREAM FROM YICHANG TO JIUJIANG, WHERE THE RIVER HEADS NORTHEAST FOR THE SEA.

◄ *A ship passes through a lock beside the Gezhouba Dam near Yichang. Before the Three Gorges Dam was started, the Gezhouba Dam was China's largest hydro-electric project, designed to produce electricity that could be carried by transmission lines as far away as Shanghai.*

AT YICHANG, the mountains and gorges are finally left behind. Downstream from Yichang, the river broadens out – in places to 1.2 miles (two kilometers) – across flat, low-lying land. This is the Yangtze's great flood plain. For centuries, flooding has been a problem here. Flood banks were built, but they were neglected and easily breached by high water. Floods along this section of the Yangtze cost 145,000 lives in 1931, 142,000 in 1935 and 30,000 in 1954. After the 1954 floods the Chinese government began a program of strengthening and raising the height of the river banks.

BUSY WATERS

Although dredgers are needed to clear the river bed and keep the Yangtze deep enough for shipping, there are no serious obstacles to ships between Yichang and the sea. The waters are busy with junks, carrying cargoes for local trade, and larger ships moving up and down river. There is industry as well as farming along this stretch of the river. Electricity from the Gezhouba Dam has made Yichang into an industrial city. About 93 miles (150 kilometers) downstream, Shashi has cotton mills, dyeworks and machinery plants. But the largest and most important of the riverside cities in this region is Wuhan, where the Yangtze is joined by the Han river. The Han, at 952 miles (1532 kilometers) long, is the Yangtze's longest tributary.

Wuhan's main industry is iron and steel-making. The city's beginnings go back nearly 2000 years. Three cities – Hankou, Hanyang and Wuchang – grew up around the meeting of the rivers, and they were later united as one. It was not until 1957 that the three cities were linked by a bridge across the Yangtze.

Hankou was a port, which specialized in the tea trade in the nineteenth century. Sailing clippers, and later steamships from Great Britain, came up the Yangtze to load cargoes of tea. Then they would race back to Britain. Tea spoils if it is too long at sea, so the fastest ships fetched the best prices. A famous sailing clipper, the *Cutty Sark*, covered a record 363 miles (584 kilometers) in one day on one of these voyages. It can still be seen at Greenwich, near London.

▲ *Tea clippers off the Chinese coast in the nineteenth century. The ship in the foreground, flying the British Red Ensign, is the* Falcon. *With their narrow hulls, sharp bows and many sails, clippers were designed for speed above all.*

THE LAKES OF THE PLAIN

As the Yangtze flows across the great plain, the landscape on both sides is dotted with hundreds of shallow lakes. The two largest are Lake Dongting, about 93 miles (150 kilometers) south of Shashi, and Lake Boyang, a further 311 miles (500 kilometers) downstream. These lakes play an important part in the life of the lower Yangtze. In summer, they act as reservoirs for the monsoon rainwater that flows into them from the hills to the south, and this helps to prevent flooding. In winter, they release the stored water and extend the farming season along the river banks.

FLOOD PREVENTION

After the flood of 1954, the Chinese government made flood prevention on the Yangtze plain an urgent priority. The 300-year-old Jingjiang Dike, stretching for 113 miles (182 kilometers) along the northern bank of the river near Shashi, was repaired and raised in height to 52 feet (sixteen meters). Elsewhere on the Yangtze and its tributaries, another 2175 miles (3500 kilometers) of river banks were strengthened, and 18,642 miles (30,000 kilometers) of channels were dug to take flood water to storage basins.

◀ *Lake Boyang on the lower Yangtze. The nature reserve on the western shore of the lake is internationally famous as the winter home of thousands of snow geese, cranes, and other migrating wildfowl.*

LAND OF FISH AND RICE

FOR THE LAST 497 MILES (800 KILOMETERS) OF ITS JOURNEY TO THE SEA, THE YANGTZE FLOWS SLOWLY ACROSS AN ALMOST LEVEL PLAIN. THIS IS CHINA'S MOST FERTILE REGION, WHERE NO SCRAP OF LAND THAT CAN BE FARMED IS WASTED.

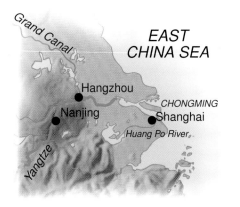

THE CHINESE CALL THIS AREA "the land of fish and rice." On the banks of the river there are networks of irrigation canals linking hundreds of shallow lakes. These are rich in freshwater fish and shellfish. Some fish breed there naturally, but other lakes are kept stocked each year to provide food for the local population. Between the lakes and waterways, fields are flooded for two rice crops in summer and then, when the floodwater drains away in autumn, farmers plant a third crop such as winter wheat. The warm, moist climate is also ideal for growing cotton, which is planted in April before the monsoon arrives and harvested in September. This leaves time for a winter crop of beans or wheat to be sown.

▲ *Planting rice near Nanjing on the lower Yangtze. Rice-growing demands a large labor force prepared to do hours of back-breaking work while standing in water.*

CHINA'S GRAIN CROPS (1995)	
Wheat:	99,297,000 tons
Rice:	175,933,000 tons
Maize:	99,275,000 tons
Sweet potatoes:	104,999,000 tons
1995 total:	479,504,000 tons
1985 total:	379,110,000 tons
1975 total:	284,565,000 tons
1965 total:	194,525,000 tons
Target for 2000:	500,000,000 tons

OLD AND NEW

The lower Yangtze shows the old China and the new side by side. Many farmers still work their land with simple tools, as they have done for hundreds of years, using oxen and water buffaloes to pull plows and carts. Large numbers of people are available to work on the rice crop – planting, weeding, irrigating and

harvesting – and they make it still profitable to farm in this way. But Yangtze farmers are turning more and more to tractors with appliances that can be attached, such as mechanical sprayers and harvesters. Because the soil of the Yangtze valley is soft, these machines must be light, and many are made in local workshops.

SIDELINES

Besides growing their main crops the farming families of the Yangtze valley increase their income with "sideline" activities. These include fish-farming, pig and poultry-keeping, growing vegetables and fruit, and rearing silkworms. Dikes and river banks are planted with mulberry trees, which provide food for the silkworms.

Over 4000 years ago, the Chinese discovered that thread could be spun from the fibers surrounding the cocoons of silkworms, the larvae of the silkmoth. Cultivating mulberry trees, rearing the moths that lay silkworm eggs and feeding the worms until the cocoons are fully grown at about six weeks old are still done on small farms. The spinning and weaving industries of lower Yangtze cities such as Nanjing, Hangzhou and Shanghai began with the manufacture of silk. These industries have developed to include cotton and, more recently, artificial fibers such as polyester produced by the petrochemical industry.

▲ *Silkworms are kept on trays and fed on fresh mulberry leaves for about six weeks before they begin to spin their cocoons. After eight days, the cocoons are removed from the trays and dried before being sent to the silk factory.*

▶ *At this silk factory in Hangzhou, cocoons are being checked for damage before the reeling process. In this process the silk fibers from up to twenty cocoons are spun together. Then this thread is spun with others to produce silk that will be ready for weaving.*

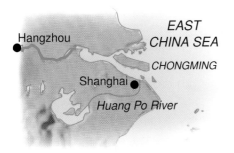

EAST
CHINA SEA

Hangzhou

CHONGMING

Shanghai

Huang Po River

THE YANGTZE DELTA

OVER THOUSANDS OF YEARS, THE ACTION
OF THE TIDES HAS CREATED THE
YANGTZE DELTA.

BELOW NANJING, the Yangtze is tidal. This means that its water level and flow are affected by the twice-daily rise and fall of the tides in the East China Sea. As the slow-flowing Yangtze approaches the sea, tidal action slows it down even more. The silt – fragments of mud and sand – in the water falls to the river bed. In the swirls and eddies of the tides, banks of silt build up, forcing the water to find a way around them. This creates a delta of marshes, sandbanks and water channels.

THE CHANGING RIVER

If it were left to nature, the delta would be in a state of constant change. New sandbanks would halt the flow of water and so it would find another route to the sea. This would leave new deposits of silt, forcing another change of direction for the river. The land would be useless for farming, and the ever-changing sandbanks would be a danger to ships going up the Yangtze because they might run aground.

Tropical cyclones, which are fierce storms beating in from the sea, can bring faster and more dramatic changes. This happened in 1852 on China's northern river, the Huang Ho. Storms and floods changed the channels and banks in the delta so much that the river found a new way to the sea 373 miles (600

▲ *The delta photographed from space. The lighter blue and light brown areas off the coast are shallows and sediments from the river. Shanghai is the brown area shown on the Huang Po river.*

kilometers) north of the old route. Deltas go on making and unmaking themselves, unless people take a hand and control the build-up of silt.

On the Yangtze, for many centuries, so many channels flowed into the sea that no one could decide which was the true river mouth. About 4000 years ago the river divided and flowed into the East China Sea through three distinct mouths. Today, there are two mouths, divided by the large island of Chongming. Where it meets the sea, the Yangtze is 57 miles (91 kilometers) wide.

SHAPING THE DELTA

As late as the beginning of the twentieth century, the delta was mostly swamp. During the summer monsoon, it was entirely under water except for a few sandbanks on which people set up temporary homes. Since then, many of the swamps have been drained. River banks have been raised, and the flood water of a normal summer is channeled away safely. But the people of the Yangtze delta still keep a close eye on water levels in the summer monsoon season. Freak floods can bring disaster.

FLOODS ON THE YANGTZE DELTA

1881: Almost one million people drowned or died of starvation.

1954: About 33,000 people drowned. Over 700,000 peasants and soldiers raced to build up the river banks against rising flood water. Even when the banks were raised the water was only eight inches (twenty centimeters) from further disaster.

1981: Over 4,000 people drowned.

1983: The river burst its banks in Anhui and Jiangsu provinces. One million people helped to carry out repairs so that autumn crops could be sown. Ninety people were drowned.

1988: Nearly 3000 people drowned.

1996: 800 people drowned.

▲ *For millions of Chinese people, bicycles are the usual form of transport. In the 1981 floods, most people had to leave their bicycles at home when they went shopping.*

SHANGHAI

SHANGHAI, CHINA'S SECOND LARGEST CITY AND ITS MAIN PORT, HAS GROWN UP BETWEEN THE MOUTH OF THE YANGTZE AND ITS LAST TRIBUTARY, THE HUANG PO.

SHANGHAI MEANS "by the sea." Over 300 years ago, it was a fortified harbor, with walls and a moat, where Chinese junks could find protection from Japanese pirates. It became an important port in the nineteenth century, and this was the start of its expansion into a huge industrial city. As it was built on the mud and silt of the Yangtze delta, the technology of the time meant that the height and weight of buildings had to be limited. So the city spread outwards instead of upwards until it became an unplanned

▲ *Shanghai's waterfront, seen from beneath the Nanpu bridge. The bridge, which opened in 1991, links Shanghai with the Pudong Development Zone across the river. It is part of Shanghai's new road system which was completed in 1995.*

sprawl. Industries such as cotton-spinning and weaving, iron and steel-making, and shipbuilding sprang up.

Shanghai's reputation for poor, overcrowded housing, bad working conditions and poor pay lasted until the 1980s. The Communist government, which ruled China from 1949, would not allow the city to spend money on modernization. Its docks and factories continued to work with outdated equipment. The roads were inadequate for a busy industrial city. The people of Shanghai

◀ *New commercial and industrial buildings in the Pudong Development Zone just outside Shanghai. The building on stilts is the 1535-foot (468-meter) high Oriental Pearl Television and Communications Center, with its circular viewing platform for visitors.*

CLEARING SHANGHAI'S SLUMS

In an effort to rid central Shanghai of overcrowding, over one million people have been moved out to ten new settlements on the Yangtze delta. These new communities have their own industrial areas, mostly connected with "new" industries, such as information technology and electronics. Meanwhile, in Shanghai itself, a $180 million (£110 million) plan was begun in 1996 to rebuild the city's water supply system and reduce pollution.

▶ *The river front, called the Bund, at Shanghai. Many of its buildings date from the nineteenth century when foreign traders set up offices there. Today, many have been converted into hotels and entertainment complexes.*

continued to live in makeshift homes that were too small for families. Then, in the 1980s, things started to change. The government agreed to let Shanghai modernize and develop.

THE NEW CITY

Today, it is hard to get away from the sight and sound of new building in Shanghai. With its new hotels, office blocks and modern shopping streets, it is a busy city. Factories have been torn down, rebuilt and equipped with up-to-date machinery. Roads, bridges and tunnels are being built. New suburbs of houses are going up. One of Shanghai's old problems – the need to bring fuel from inland China – has been solved in the last twenty years by the building of power transmission lines from the hydroelectric station at the Gezhouba Dam. Special areas of the city have been earmarked for new industries and activities. The huge Baoshan Iron and Steel Complex, one of the first results of Shanghai's

new prosperity, is to be expanded still further. The suburb of Caohejing has been chosen as the site of new electronic industries, such as the manufacture of microchips.

Most important of all, Shanghai is aiming to win back its old reputation as China's "gateway to the world." China has one of the fastest growing economies in the world. In 1995 its exports increased by almost 23 per cent and its imports by over 14 per cent from the previous year, which was itself a record. Shanghai is a key city in China's drive to increase exports to $147 billion (£90 billion) in the year 2000. A special area, the Pudong Development Zone, is being built to the east of the city, with container and bulk cargo docks and banking and trading centers to cope with the increase in trade.

THE MONSOON

LIFE ON THE YANGTZE DEPENDS ON THE MONSOON — THE SUMMER SEASON OF HEAVY RAINSTORMS THAT SWEEP IN FROM THE SEA.

THE MOVEMENT OF THE MONSOON is caused by changes in atmospheric pressure. In spring, the land mass of Asia begins to warm up more quickly than the sea. Hot air over the land rises, creating an area of low pressure beneath it. Meanwhile, over the sea, high pressure builds up in the cool, moist air. When the monsoon "breaks," this cool air, laden with moisture from the ocean, sweeps into the low-pressure area from the southeast. It brings weeks of torrential rain, often accompanied by fierce thunderstorms.

UNCERTAIN RAINS

In a normal year, the monsoon arrives in the lower reaches of the Yangtze in April. From then

▲ *Boats took to the streets in Jiangsu province in 1981 after the extreme flooding. The monsoon that year was heavy and long-lasting, so that rain was still pouring down on the lower Yangtze when the first floodwater arrived from upstream.*

on the area of the heaviest rain gradually moves westwards, arriving in the Sichuan Basin in late July. For example, Yichang has 3.8 inches (98 millimeters) of rain in an average April, rising to almost 8 inches (205 millimeters) in July, then falling to 7 inches (175 millimeters) in August. In comparison, in the rainiest parts of Great Britain on the western side of the country, the wettest month is January with a typical rainfall of 6 inches (150 millimeters).

34

Although the monsoon is more predictable than the weather systems of temperate zones such as western Europe, this is not always so. Sometimes the monsoon travels faster than usual. Normally, the lower and middle sections of the Yangtze are hit by the monsoon rain before the monsoon reaches the river to the west. Similarly, the low-lying land of the Sichuan Basin normally receives its rainfall before the upper Yangtze and its tributaries. In the Sichuan Basin and on the lower Yangtze, a normal year's floodwater – about 82 feet (25 meters) at Chongqing – is controlled by the system of banks, irrigation channels and overflow reservoirs that store surplus water. But if the monsoon moves too quickly, bringing rain to the whole river within a short time, there is too much floodwater for the system to cope with. The result is a disastrous flood downstream. This was what happened in 1981 and again in 1984 when floods drowned thousands of people in Sichuan and on the Yangtze delta.

There is no way of forecasting the behavior of the monsoon or the chance of flooding, but, on average, floods happen along the Yangtze about once every ten years. Sometimes they are more frequent, as they were in the early 1980s. When engineers are planning flood-prevention plans, they use a calculation based on the frequency of serious floods. A "one-in-ten-year" flood happens fairly often. The flood of 1954, which killed 30,000 people and left nineteen million homeless, was rated as a "one-in-50-year" flood.

WHEN THE MONSOON FAILS

Even more serious than flooding is the failure of the monsoon to appear at all. This not only brings untold misery and hardship to the people of the Yangtze, but also spreads food shortages throughout China. Fortunately, it does not happen often. This last happened on the Yangtze in the terrible years of 1876 to 1879 when the monsoon failed to arrive summer after summer. Between nine and thirteen million Chinese people died of starvation.

▲ *Barges unload stone to build up flood banks in Sichuan. Local people were once expected to keep their flood banks in good repair, but they often neglected their duty. Today, flood prevention is better organized.*

FLOOD LEVELS

Floods rarely affect the whole of the Yangtze in any one year. The figures below show the maximum height of floodwater at Yichang in flood years. For Yichang, the level reached in 1870 and 1981 would be calculated as a 'one-in-100-year' flood.

Year	Height	
1796	2204 in	(5600 cm)
1860	2283 in	(5800 cm)
1870	2323 in	(5900 cm)
1896	2204 in	(5600 cm)
1954	2244 in	(5700 cm)
1981	2323 in	(5900 cm)
1984	2204 in	(5600 cm)

CHINA'S LIFELINE

WITH OVER 1000 MILLION PEOPLE, CHINA IS THE MOST HEAVILY
POPULATED COUNTRY IN THE WORLD. THROUGHOUT HISTORY,
THE PRIORITY FOR CHINESE PEOPLE HAS ALWAYS
BEEN TO GROW ENOUGH FOOD TO LIVE.

ONLY ABOUT TEN PER
CENT OF CHINA'S LAND
is suitable for
farming, but 60
per cent of Chinese
people work on the
land. Many of them
work on small farms
without the help of
modern machinery
or methods, which
explains the very
high proportion of
farm workers compared with more mechanized
agricultural countries. "Will there be enough
to eat?" is the question that always hangs over
China, which has only ten per cent of the
world's farmland to feed twenty per cent of the
world's population. The Sichuan Basin alone
grows the food that supports 33 per cent of
China's people.

◀ *A peasant
farmer brings home
the rice harvest. For
millions of farmers
like him, an ox-cart
is still the favored
form of transport.*

FAMILY FARMS

There are no vast farms in China covering
thousands of acres as there are in the United
States and Russia. One of the first actions of
the new Communist government in 1949 was
to take land away from rich landlords and
hand it to the peasants. The peasants were
organized into groups of villages, called
collectives, which were given targets for each
of their crops. But this system did not work,
partly because there was no extra reward for
the peasants who worked hardest. In the ten
years before the peasants were given back

their land in 1984, grain production
increased by just over two per cent per year. In
the next ten years the increase per year was
nearly four per cent.

Most farmers grow a mixture of subsistence
crops – food grown for themselves – and cash
crops, which they sell. Besides rice and wheat,
the cash crops include sugar-cane, fruit,
vegetables and cotton.

A VITAL
TRANSPORT ROUTE

The Yangtze is a lifeline in other ways too.
Until the beginning of the twentieth century,
it provided the only route into the middle of
China. All the produce of the Sichuan Basin
had to travel down the river before it could
be distributed elsewhere in China or sold
abroad. Although railways have reduced the
importance of river trade, it should flourish
again when the Three Gorges Project is
completed and sailing upriver as far as

CROPS ON THE YANGTZE

Proportions of China's national needs produced along the Yangtze:

Rice:	70 per cent
Grain:	40 per cent
Cotton:	35 per cent
Freshwater fish:	50 per cent

▲ *A good catch of huang chuang for these fishermen. The huang chuang, sometimes called the dog salmon, is a member of the carp family and can weigh up to 132 pounds (60 kilograms).*

▼ *A tourist cruiser on the Yangtze. In 1995 over 46 million people visited China. After the Great Wall and Beijing, the Three Gorges is the third most popular area.*

Chongqing is possible for large cargo ships.

The lakes of the lower Yangtze and the delta are well stocked with fish, both naturally and by fish-farming. Waste from fish caught for food is used as fertilizer and animal feed.

ENERGY POTENTIAL

The other great potential of the Yangtze and its tributaries is as a source of energy. In 1995 only two per cent of China's energy came from hydroelectricity. Eight hydroelectric power stations are already operating in China and another ten, including the Three Gorges Project, are being built. There are plans for over twenty more. China's expanding economy will lead to a huge increase in the demand for energy, but it will also provide money to pay for energy development.

THREATS TO THE YANGTZE

A LONG RIVER LIKE THE YANGTZE FLOWS THROUGH MANY DIFFERENT ENVIRONMENTS. MANY THINGS CAN HAPPEN TO IT ALONG ITS COURSE. SOME OF THESE THINGS HAPPEN NATURALLY. OTHERS ARE THE RESULT OF HUMAN ACTIVITY.

FARMING AND EROSION

IN THE SICHUAN BASIN, farmers have cleared wooded hillsides and planted crops on them. Trees absorb rainfall and let it trickle slowly into the earth. When hillsides are cleared, water running off the slopes in the rainy season carries soil with it. The land becomes poorer and less able to support good crops. Meanwhile the soil that is eroded flows into rivers and lakes, increasing the risk of flooding and interfering with carefully planned irrigation projects.

In the past 30 years, the area of land in the Yangtze valley damaged by soil erosion has doubled, and in the Sichuan Basin it has increased by four times.

The Chinese government is trying to stop further damage. One way is to replant the slopes with trees so that farmers can make a living by growing fruit, or mulberry trees for silkworms. Another answer is to turn the slopes into grazing land for herds of animals. Grass roots help to bind the soil together and keep it in place.

A third solution is to terrace the slopes instead of farming them as sloping fields. Terraces are narrow, flat surfaces of soil kept in place by walls or earth banks. Because they are flat, rainwater seeps down through them instead of washing the soil away.

PLANT A TREE

The entire Chinese population is involved in a government reforestation program aimed at restoring China's trees. Everyone over the age of eleven has to plant at least three trees a year or take part in other reforestation work, such as preparing the ground or tending the young trees. Trees are being planted in towns and cities as well as in the countryside. The aim is to increase the area of China's forests by twenty per cent by the year 2000. By 2040 China hopes to grow enough timber for its own needs.

▲ *Terracing enables sloping land to be farmed without risking soil erosion. These terraced paddy fields are supplied with water from a tributary of the Yangtze that has been diverted.*

TRAPPED IN THE DAMS

Some experts are worried about how soil erosion will affect the Gezhouba Dam and the Three Gorges Dam. They fear that the dams will trap deposits and, in future years, raise the water in the reservoirs behind the dams to dangerous levels. The pressure of the deposits might even cause the dams to burst, with disastrous results for the people who live downstream. Other engineers say that only

clear water is to be stored in the reservoirs, and the sediments will be washed away downstream. But even this will interfere with the natural behavior of the river. It may be many years before anyone is proved right.

POLLUTION IN THE CITIES

China's older heavy industries such as iron and steelmaking use mainly coal as fuel, and the air in industrial centers like Chongqing, Nanjing and Shanghai is often thick with fumes. Spare ground and even canals have been used as dumps for chemical and industrial waste. But since 1990 the government has been urging industry to cut pollution by modernizing its methods of waste disposal.

▲ *Industrial haze over Shanghai. China ignored the problem of industrial pollution for many years, but it is now coming into line with international standards of pollution control.*

▲ *Waste pulp from papermaking on the Grand Canal looks unsightly, but it will disperse and eventually rot in the water.*

◄ *Shanghai's waste is transported by barge downstream for dumping.*

CONSERVATION ON THE YANGTZE

INTENSIVE FARMING AND HUMAN SETTLEMENT IN THE YANGTZE
VALLEY HAVE STRIPPED IT OF MOST OF ITS NATURAL WILDLIFE.
BUT IN THE LAKES OF THE LOWER YANGTZE, THE MOUNTAINS
OF WESTERN SICHUAN AND THE UPPER REACHES OF THE
RIVER, RARE PLANT AND ANIMAL LIFE STILL SURVIVES.

ENDANGERED SPECIES

THE FORESTS AND HIGH PLATEAU of the upper
Yangtze and its tributaries are home to many
endangered species. Among these is the snow
leopard, one of the six species of large cats,
weighing between 110 and 154 pounds (50
and 70 kilograms). Its coat was highly prized
in the fur trade, and it was hunted almost to
extinction. It is near the top of the United
Nations list of endangered species and
officially protected, but still hunted illegally.
The number of surviving snow leopards is
unknown, but experts think that it is no more
than two or three hundred.

Altogether in China, 40 species of
mammals, 83 species of birds and 350 plants
are listed as endangered. Although a small
number of national parks, covering 0.2 per
cent of China's land, have been set up, they
are often in remote areas where it is difficult
to control illegal hunting.

An approach the government has adopted
for saving rare plants is to collect the plants
from threatened areas, such as the Three
Gorges Dam area, and transplant them in new
habitats.

CONSERVING FISH STOCKS

Fish are one of the important resources of the
lower Yangtze and its lakes. The river from
Chongqing to Lake Dongting, for example, is a

▲ *The few surviving snow leopards in the world
live in the mountains of western China. They live
near the snowline, coming down to the forests in
autumn. Snow leopards hunt on their own at night
for deer, sheep, goats, smaller mammals and birds.*

major breeding ground for four species of carp
as well as more common fish. Some biologists
are worried that hydroelectric projects on the
Yangtze will threaten these species. Carp and
sturgeon – a species that is endangered and
therefore protected by the state – feed from the
river bed. Changes in the sediment on the river
bed could deprive them of their natural food.

Damming the Yangtze also could threaten
migrating fish species, which breed in the
upper reaches and then move downstream.

40

THE GIANT PANDA

The Chinese government's best-known attempt at conservation is its effort to save the giant panda from extinction. This large black and white bear-like raccoon, weighing up to 308 pounds (140 kilograms), lives in the wild in only one now protected habitat, the bamboo forests on the western edge of the Sichuan Basin. Bamboo shoots are its main source of food. Destruction of the bamboo thickets was already a threat to the giant panda when, in the late 1970s, large areas of bamboo flowered and died. Many pandas starved, and there are now thought to be fewer than 400 in the wild. Chinese zoologists have begun a breeding program in the hope that one day the number of pandas will again be on the increase.

YANGTZE FLORA

Many of the plants in parks and gardens around us originally came from China. The warm, temperate Sichuan Basin is the true home of plants such as rhododendrons, azaleas, primulas, peonies, camellias, buddleia and regal lilies. All the examples of these grown in Western countries are descendants of specimens brought out of China by nineteenth-century botanists. Many of the hillsides where these shrubs flourished have since been cultivated, but others still provide a colorful display in the late spring and summer. Some species, including azaleas and rhododendrons, spread so quickly that they can overwhelm cultivated slopes unless they are kept under control.

◀ *The Jiuzhaigou nature reserve in northern Sichuan is one of China's largest and in the forefront of China's conservation policy. It protects an area that has been untouched by industry or forestry.*

THE FUTURE

CHINA PLANS TO ENTER THE 21ST CENTURY WITH A STANDARD OF LIVING THAT CAN COMPETE WITH THE WORLD'S LEADING INDUSTRIAL NATIONS. VAST CHANGES HAVE TAKEN PLACE SINCE 1980, AND MORE ARE ON THE WAY.

UNTIL 1980, China was mainly concerned with the problems it faced after almost a century of revolution, war and civil war. In 1949, when a Communist government came to power, China was in ruins. Millions of people were on the verge of starvation. Factories and machinery had been destroyed in the fighting. War meant that China had missed out on most of the technological and social changes of the twentieth century. Only about ten per cent of its population had received any education. There was one doctor for every 30,000 people and one hospital for every 1.3 million.

NEW IDEAS

China struggled to bring itself up to date, mainly without outside help. But then, in 1980, there was a change of leadership and a change of ideas. China had been suspicious of Western countries. Now, it began to welcome and encourage Western investment, Western technology and Western imports. Foreign companies were invited into China to set up factories and train local people to manage and operate them. Chinese-owned factories were re-equipped with the latest machinery. For the first time, tourists were welcomed, bringing with them Western money. By 1990, China had agreed with Japan, after years of rivalry, on a loan to pay for new roads, harbors, railways and power stations.

SHIFTING THE BALANCE

Another change in government thinking helped the Yangtze in particular. Before 1980, the river had been neglected. Little government money went into projects along the Yangtze. Just as the changes brought new life to Shanghai, so they brought investment into the Yangtze valley. The huge hydro-electricity program is just one example. The government had come to realize that the Yangtze was a resource for the whole of China, not just for the people who lived next to it.

◀ In November 1996, Chinese and British representatives signed the contract for the building of the Jiangyin Bridge over the Yangtze, 93 miles (150 kilometers) upstream from Shanghai. The 4544-foot (1385-meter) suspension bridge will be high enough for ocean-going ships to pass underneath.

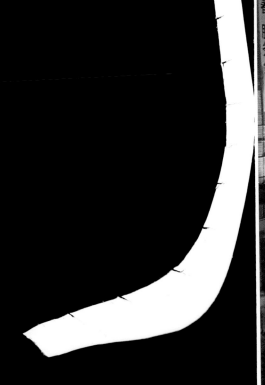

▲ *Busy shops, bright lights, and, of course, traffic problems are now as familiar in Shanghai as in any city in the Western world. Shanghai was the first city to benefit from the government's policy of offering an "open door" to the rest of the world.*

EVERYDAY LIFE

Change in China has affected the lives of everyone. There is now a school place for almost every Chinese child, and a doctor for every 1000 people.

Radios, television sets and other electrical goods are imported from Japan and southern Asia or made in China by foreign companies. In the fifteen years from 1980 to 1995, the number of television sets in China rose ten times, from 2.5 million to 25 million.

So far, it is people who live in China's towns and cities who have gained most from the changes in China. Most of the people who live along the Yangtze are farmers, still struggling to make a living. Perhaps, in time, they will be able to share in their country's new prosperity.

▲ *The rising standard of living in Shanghai is shown by the growth of fashion shops selling designer clothes, many made by international companies which have set up factories in China.*

GLOSSARY

bulk cargo one particular type of cargo carried loose in the hold of a ship

cash crop a crop that the farmer grows to sell

civil war war between people who live in the same country

collective a group of people who work together for the good of their community

container cargo a cargo made up of goods packed into metal containers

course (of a river) the path of a river between its source and its mouth

crust the outer layer of the Earth's surface

crustal plates pieces of the outer layer of the Earth's surface

delta flat land at the mouth of a river made up of sand and mud

dike a bank built beside the sea or a river to prevent flooding

dredger a ship that clears sand and mud from the river or sea bed

eddy a swirling current in water which makes a small whirlpool

false-color satellite image a photograph taken from space that uses unnatural colors to highlight certain features

forestry planting and managing trees as a crop

generator a machine that converts steam or water power into electricity

glacier a moving sheet of thick ice

gulf a large, deep bay

hydroelectric power energy produced by converting the energy of falling water into electricity

intensive cultivation the use of land for as much produce as possible

irrigation distributing water to fields by pipes or canals

junk a flat-bottomed boat with a square sail

jute a plant whose fiber is used to make sacks and rope

larva the stage in the development of some insects between the egg and the adult form

meltwater melted snow or ice

mouth (of a river) the place where a river meets the sea

nomads people who move from place to place to find food for themselves and their animals

paddy field a field that is flooded for the planting of rice

petrochemical industry the manufacture of chemicals from oil

province part of a country that has its own local government

ravine a narrow, steep-sided valley

reaches sections of a river

reforestation planting forest trees

reservoir a natural or artificial lake used for storing water

sediment soil, sand and small pieces of rock that are caught up in the flow of a river and later sink to the river bed

ship elevators lifts that carry ships over obstructions

silt muddy sediment

snowcap the covering of snow on top of a mountain

subsistence crop a crop grown for the farmer's own use

temperate mild; neither very hot nor very cold

tributary a smaller river that flows into a large river